WHERE IT HAPPENED

For Jayne —

Best wishes on a beautiful
February afternoon. I hope
you enjoy these poems.
  Take Care,
    Ben

Where It Happened

ℭ

poems by
Benjamin Gotschall

Benjamin D. Gotschall
2/12/09

Sandhills Press
Scotia, Nebraska / Nacogdoches, Texas

Published by:
Sandhills Press
Mark Sanders, Editor and Publisher
lcpublishing@hotmail.com

ISBN: 0-911015-60-4
978-0-911015-60-7

Cover design and layout by Sean Watkins and Mark Sanders.
Cover photography © 2006 Timmy Samuel, www.starbellystudios.com

Manufactured in the United States of America

Acknowledgments:

I would like to thank the editors of the following publications in which these poems, sometimes in earlier versions, first appeared: *Meridian*, "Heat"; *Cimarron Review*, "Team Roping"; *South Dakota Review*, "At the Auto Shop"; *Poetry Southeast*, "Cherries"; *The Meadow*, "Idaho"; *Nimrod*, "Grasshoppers"; *Best New Poets 2007*, "Bait"; and, *Cadence of Hooves: A Celebration of Horses*, "Riding to Work."

Many thanks to Mark Sanders at Sandhills Press, and to my M.F.A. thesis committee members at the University of Idaho: Robert Wrigley, Joy Passanante, and Joseph Guenthner. Their time, effort and input has been greatly valued and appreciated.

Gratitude is also extended to William Kloefkorn, Annie Berical, Dan Berkner, Todd Imus, Sam Renken, and Sue Renken.

Last, but certainly not least, I would like to recognize the sacrifices made, support given, and prayers sent up by my family, especially by my mother, father, brothers and sisters. You've all done more than you know to give me a place to return to, even if only in my mind, that is always home.

For my family,
and for my grandfather, Dean Gotschall,
in memory

Contents

The Sandhills cover an area of nearly 20,000 square miles, or about a quarter of the state's total area. They also represent the nearest thing to true wilderness area anywhere in the United States east of the Rockies, to say nothing of supporting the largest intact area of mixed-grass prairie that still survives south of Canada.

—Paul Johnsgard

One of the last regions tapped by the range-hungry cattlemen was one of the best—the sandhills of Nebraska, a great egg-shaped region blown in on an old lake bed . . . Except for the narrow border of low chophills all around, the region was a series of high, generally grassed parallel ridges running southeastward, the tops of the highest wind-torn, sand flying from an occasional blowout, altogether like a great sea running, with here and there a crest to break . . . Altogether the sandhills were one great sponge. With no runoff water, every drop of moisture soaked in, to follow the shallow water table that formed the lakes, and, as the land fell away, seeped out in little veinings of clear, steady streams that grew and headed southeastward for the Platte. Ranches had crept up the lower reaches of these streams even before the moccasin of the Indian was gone . . .

—Mari Sandoz

ARROWHEAD

I found it resting in the sand
of a wind-swept blowout,
near rain-washed yucca roots
uncovered by a recent storm.

I noticed first its fine point, then
the feathered edges flaked from stone
by hands long dead.

Between thumb and forefinger I felt the notches
sinew once wrapped to shaft. I held it
to the sun. Light passed through
as if through stained glass

the color of blood, what blood
it may have shed sunk deeper
than memory into earth.

Part I

My mind moves in more than one place,
In a country half-land, half-water . . .

What I love is near at hand,
Always, in earth and air.

—Theodore Roethke

ADOPTION

Because his mother died, and because that cow
lost this one, Dad says as he cuts
around the knob of each knee,
along each leg, down the center
of the dead calf's white belly.

He gives the knife to me. At first
I grasp it like a baseball bat, then
between thumb and forefinger
as I follow the grooves
of the antler handle.

Dad peels the skin away from the muscles,
yellow stains of fat blotching
the map of veins.
With lengths of baling twine,
he lashes the red hide

to the orphan calf's black back
and turns him in with the Hereford cow.
Pacing the fence, she stops,
eyes wide as she watches him
wobble toward her.

The calf butts
her swollen udder. She lowers
her muzzle, sniffs the cape
and looks at us
looking at her.

The curve of sky between her horns
rocks with the pitch of her head
as she licks a spit-dark whorl
into the dead hair
and lets her milk down.

Skinny Dipping

We race to Holt Creek,
throw our clothes
behind us in trails.
My bare feet flinch
atop prickly-tipped, cattle-cropped grass,
and I jump off the bank
into tea-colored water,
come up with hair in my eyes,
frog-swim to the shallow.
My toes wriggle in the cool sand

as I walk, minnows flit
in confusion, transparent bodies
tapping my ankles.
When I step onto hot-dry-white,
powdered grains stick to my soles,
my brother splashes in behind me,
and I swim out to wrestle him,
dunking us both
coughing and laughing,
creekwater and snot boiling out my nose.

He runs to the shore
where I tackle him onto the hot-dry-white,
our glistening bodies caked.
He escapes, stoops,
scoops a handful. Gray glop
oozes through fingers, streaks dark
down his forearms. He slings
a scattered pattern of slop
that stings my turned cheek
and pocks my neck and chest.

After the mudfight,
crab-walking the creekbottom,
my hands grasp plants,
pull toward the bank until
I crawl out tired,
drip and dress in the bluegrass,
my sun-soaked socks
warming my wrinkled toes.
We walk to the house,
our clothes moisture-snug.

During my turn in the tub,
washing the sand
out of my hair,
ears and crack, the grains
scour my skin smooth,
become my flesh, and rinse me
down the drain and back
into Holt Creek, where I rise again,
naked, baptized,and clean.

DIGGING OUT THE HOUND

for my brother Marcus

The yellow globe of lantern-glow
hung from my father's fingers
as he looked first at the hole that led
under the abandoned farmhouse, then
at me. *The 'coon is in the wall,* he said, *the dog
can't turn around.* He pulled his pliers
from a pouch at his belt. *This is all we've got
to dig with,* he told me, and held it out.
You're small enough to fit.

Through the crawlspace, I followed
the beam of the flashlight in my mouth
toward the sound of claws
scraping wood. I plunged the pliers'
pointed head into the ground. Above,
boards creaked. The night
was steel in my hand, smell
of fur and dirt.
Every shadow had teeth.

DIVE

I'm looking at dandelions
on the tee-ball diamond built
in the wrong place
for rightfielders
with no sunglasses.

We're playing the Twins,
and they're tough, but
the kid with the cast just came up,
and he swings
with one arm.

Since I'm out here, I'm closer
to the park with the squeaky swings
and the red tornado slide, closer
to the pool, which is cooler
than this.

If the game's over soon,
I'll have enough time
to work on my cannonball,
and there will still be
enough daylight
to stay warm while wet.

A monarch butterfly
as big as a wren
flutters too close,
almost within glove-
slapping distance,
then

the diving board claps, masks
the sound of the bat,
and the pop fly hides itself
in the blinding gold
of the sun.

The dull thud that chunks the grass
is me missing the catch, wanting
to be a seal diving, sliding
into the green deep
without a splash.

HEAT

After Linda Bierds

The bedding hay nested
the bow of her ribs, and no lower.
Hooks, thurls, the ridge of her chine,
warm. All night she lay
in the snowscape pasture,
her cow-eyes closed from the wind.
By morning she was dead.
Heat, I learned—not freezing—
killed her, the rumen fluid
upturned in the downhill stomach
flowing with acid, eating the heart.
I had come from the house, where driven snow
slouched a single sled-slope against doorways
and eaves. When I came back
she had rolled, only the points of her hooves
breaking the drift. I remember wind,
a dark red cave,
and the yipping of fat coyotes
licking each other's bloody shoulders.

HAYFIELD, LATE JULY

"Some year we'll have perfect hay."
—William Stafford

Late July in the Sandhills means prayer.
The corn farmers north of town pray
for rain enough to keep their center-
pivots still, my dad asks God
for one more dry day to finish
putting up all that grass *à la mowed.*

This late July, I make windrows of second-
cutting red clover, my dad makes bales
to feed the milk cows in winter.
What's left over will bring
good money from the neighbors
whose barrel-racing and calf-roping horses
eat better than they do.

I'm wearing cutoff jeans
and dirty white canvas sneakers, and the sun
has bronzed my body to rust.
As the fragrant crackle of dried prairie
mingles with the floating, dusty dragonflies
to suspend the afternoon air, I think
about last night
when the team and I dressed
for the Ainsworth game:

Lacey Haversham in the bleachers watched
as I led off, got on base with a slap single,
stole second, rounded third,
and scored the first run. I smiled
at her from the dugout, and I smile

even now, six windrows ahead,
when the first cold drops shiver
my bare back and sprinkle tires
of the tractor, the scent of rain
heavy, lightning on the horizon.

I look to see Dad with his knife
cutting spongy stems of timothy
to unplug the baler. He waves *Stop*. I pull
the hand clutch, unplug the battery,
slide the rusty sauerkraut can over
the tractor's hot muffler and drive the pickup
to the other side of the field.

Dad scoots me over,
cursing six wasted windrows
we won't be able to cure again
because I got too far ahead.
His fist punctuates his last angry sentence.
The windshield crunches like puddled ice.
The drive back carries the silent charge
of the storm outside the window,
building.

Top price for that hay would be Mom
not frowning at the checkbook.
100 tons at 75 would be Dad not scratching his head
when the gas tanks run dry. For him, late July
means prayer, wet windrows
anger. He's not mad at me,
but at the dark clouds, which open
and pour, late July's prayers
answered by huge drops
pounding the pickup roof like fists.

WHERE IT HAPPENED

I knew something was wrong
when I saw the fear on Uncle Curt's
whiskered face and heard his voice
quiver when he said
he didn't want to load another kid
into an ambulance that day.

On the way to town later I saw
where it happened:
fresh-tilled tire tracks and a trail
of broken posts and barbed-
wire led through matted cattails
down into ditchwater

about a hundred yards south
of the one-room schoolhouse
where in a couple of months
I would start eighth grade—
the one she
had just finished.

It wasn't the first time a kid from out south
couldn't keep it between the shoulders,
but this time
a creosote-treated log
had to jump in and ruin everything.

Dad said she hit the thick gravel
in front of Fred's mailbox, crossed
to the east ditch, took out Bruce's fence
and ramped over the road
into the rushes.

She wasn't driving with beer-
blurred vision or swerving
to miss Hank's sheep
or a deer. She was taking food
to the hay crew,
and she was late.

Uncle Curt said the baked beans
burned her all over,
and when he got to the part
about the fence post that came
through the windshield,
he stopped.

He closed his eyes,
but I could tell he was thinking
of her face, because at the service
I saw it. It wasn't the one I picked
to be on my kickball team at recess,

and it wasn't the one
I sat next to at 4-H meetings,
and it wasn't the one I remembered
looking in,
but it's the one I remember
looking back.

It's the one I remember
every time my foot hits the brake
a mile before that place
where the marsh grass
never grew back the same.

AT THE AUTO SHOP

While other kids my age
hear the second bell
of the first period
of Monday morning classes
at West Holt High School,
Mom drops me off
on the east side of the shop.

I did my lessons last night
at home, watched the videos that come
every two weeks from Pensacola,
memorized by rote the preamble
to the Constitution, *We the People of the United States,*
fell asleep on my notebook in a puddle
of drool blurring the blue ruling, and woke up

from a dream as I was about to form
a more perfect union with the redhead in the centerfold
of the *Playboy* next to the can
at the auto shop.
After securing her blessings of liberty,
she told me to *Wake up,*
Wake up, in a voice that became my mother's
from the top of the stairs,
stirring me in the sweaty sheets
of my basement bed.

At the auto shop,
Don tells me Lacey Haversham
left her school car in for service,
so with one hand I grasp
a 9/16" wrench, with the other

a keychain bearing the letters L,O, V and E
on each leaf of a green plastic clover.
I think I love Lacey.

I don't know why. Perhaps
the way her first name evokes the mystery
of women's undergarments, or the rhythm
of her second name—*Haversham*—
the emphasis on the first syllable,
reminding me that I want to have her,
and that I don't,
because I can't,
or that I haven't yet,
as I haven't yet kissed a girl
or even held hands.

Neither have I tasted beer, but I smell
its stale sourness on stained floor mats;
nor tried cigarettes, their dusty smoke
emanating from seat fabric
as I park Lacey's car in the shop,
where I promote its general welfare,
take out the radiator to fix the leak,
change the oil filter, check fluids,
belts and hoses. I replace worn brake pads
to provide for the common defense.

To insure domestic tranquility
between Lacey and her dad,
I vacuum ashtrays, spray the dash
with Armor-All, and wash what might be vomit
off the window and the inside of the door,
wondering the whole while
where the party was, if she went
with one of the older boys
or with her girlfriends.

When Lacey arrives for her car, she opens the office door,
smiles, and holds out her hand for the keys,
and as my black-nailed, knuckle-bruised,
grease-stained, calloused fingers drop them into it, I feel
the brief brush of her palm, so soft,
pink and warm it seems
like it couldn't be that clean.

CHERRIES

It's what the senior football players call girls
who haven't done it yet, naming them
after what the senior guys are after—
to get one for the first time, before
anybody else, to brag
behind locker room walls
as if it were something to pin
to a letter jacket or dangle
from a rear-view mirror.

I sit in a towel, my feet hot
on cool tile, and listen to Rusty Miller brag
about what he did after the game Friday night:
Lacey Haversham, whose fifteen-freckled nose
and green eyes I long for every day fourth period—
Lacey, who, by sharing a lab tray, makes me
a better biologist. For her
I would dissect a dozen dead frogs
just so she wouldn't have to touch
even one.

I wonder if she felt she had to touch Rusty
in the bench seat of his Chevy. I wonder
if the older cheerleaders told her
what he would be like, that he would tell
the whole football team
the color of her panties,
the noises she made,
how she felt, that he wouldn't kick her out
of bed for eating crackers.

Rusty strides out of the shower, jokes
naked with the quarterback and the left tackle, says
Bet you wish your dick's been half the places mine has,
and, drying it off, says something
about a new record, something
about cherries, and I think of summers,

how I picked them for Grandma Betty
in the trees down by the garden:
each one placed in a Blue Bunny ice-
cream bucket, each one baked
into pie, each one savored
on the tongue, their sour-sweet warmth
mingled with cool vanilla
melting at the spoon's edge. I think
of second-period English class,
Odysseus in the land
of the Lotus eaters. No amount of opium
could tempt me from returning
the spoon to my lips, the taste
still on my tongue as I picture Lacey

on the bench seat of Rusty's Chevy,
moonlight, her red-brown hair
and slender body against his
fullback's shoulders, his long
linebacker's arms. I imagine her dressing
while he takes a piss and grabs
another beer, and I wonder
what it would have been like
to have been him then. I wonder
what kind of taste
it would leave in her mouth
if she knew what she was worth
behind locker room walls.

First Time

Makin' love is like milkin' a cow--
it's all about the approach, the sign
hanging on the wall reads
in handwritten scrawl.
That's what my old man used to tell me, anyway,
Don Milnar says
from behind the scarred-up desk
in the office of Atkinson Automotive Center.

Sitting on the NAPA stool in the corner
by the parts catalogs, I take a sip
of my Royal Crown Cola and laugh
because Dad does. He laughs
because he understands, because
he's a dairyman,
but he isn't laughing

nine years later, when the just-fresh
Holstein, her cantaloupe udder
tight with colostrum, attempts to escape from the holding pen.
It's her first time, blinking
under the fluorescent parlor bulbs, and she's nervous
about the vacuum pump's pulsating rhythm,
and the older ones have crowded her, butted her,
showed her who's boss, and when she tries to squeeze
between the iron doorpost
and the barn, she doesn't get it right.

Lodged between hook-bone and rib-cage,
struggling to get free, trapped
by her postpartum swell,
she's not only going nowhere fast,

but getting there early. Dad pokes her,
prods her, cracks a scoop-shovel handle
across her back, but she won't budge. Just short
of reaching for the rifle,
he reaches for the come-along winch, and together,
with a log chain, we pull her out of that tight space,
just as we pulled her stout calf from her womb, slimy,
limp-legged, sniffling and blinking
into his world's first light
three hours ago.

We finish chores and feed the newborn bull
a bottle of his mother's milk, and when I pour
the dab he didn't drink into a hubcap for the barncats,
the gray striped tom shows up
with the snelled barb
of a treble fish-hook
deep inside the roof of his mouth.

While Dad holds the tomcat, I hold
the cool silver handle of the needle-
nosed Vise-Grips steady, lock the handle,
angle the shaft of the hook and push,
the slightly sickening release
like the time I pulled out
my front tooth at recess
after Vance Garwood's chest-pass
across the lane hit me
square on the mouth.

Later that night,
in the fervent repose
of a Pontiac's backseat, my fingers
fumble unfamiliar buttons as I try
to make my mouth kiss her

good enough so she won't notice
my hands have no clue
what they are about to do.

APOLOGY DUE

To the young pregnant woman
who stood in the doorway
that October and watched
as I, unaware, snatched the jack o' lantern
carved menacingly and resting
on the redwood steps:

I did not mean to trip
over the yard gnome
reclined on his toadstool
sipping his stein of stone foam,
nor to stagger
through your marigolds, my feet
trapped in their pot of peat, planting me
on the concrete driveway,
where my fall, broken
by a hollow squash,
struck you as funny, and you said
Serves you right, you little sonofabitch,
as I lay there,
looked up and saw you,
your belly a pumpkin
as you pointed and laughed.

COMMUNION

I've visited almost every brand
of church around, like I visit this one
today. I've knelt with Catholics, said
a Southern Baptist *Amen*, shaken
Methodist hands to *Peace be with you*, and also
with Lutherans, and it always felt like
the clip-on tie I wear now, borrowed
from my buddy Justin this morning.
I stayed at his house last night
after we got drunk at a keg party
where we shared the same cup.

This time the man with the silver tray
of white wafers in his hand
is Gordon Dodd, who owns the grazing range
adjacent to our ranch. As I approach,
he sees me and shakes his head, his expression
sad. He passes me by. I know
he would have let me
if he hadn't known
who I am,
so I turn and take this
in remembrance:

My father used to be the Dodd ranch
hired man. He calved out cows, put up hay
and built tight fences. Gordon was my tee-
ball coach when I was seven, got pneumonia
and missed the first three games. He sent me
a get-well card. Once, his son Darrin threw me
a fifteen-yard pass for a first down
during a junior high football game.

I sit down in the back pew next to Justin. After
A Closer Walk with Thee and a prayer,
I file outside with everyone else. The wide
street stretches out in front of us:
Affiliated Foods on the left, Township Library
on the right. A row of cars
lines each curb, and the sun
glaring off all those windows
for a moment leaves me blind.

GOODBYE

We try to make the most
of this last night's blackness,
but this last night just might
be that. You'll find things—
new things, more things,
your things—and those things
will fall into place.

Maybe sometimes you will come
back to this night
beside this lake, and a minute
will take you to me
and the lights
going by on the highway.

Your hair reflecting
the moon's reflected
eye falls over
our faces,
in our mouths,
and you sweep it away.

Your shoulders, shivers
of warmth in this cool stillness,
press against mine, and maybe
someday you'll remember
my fingers along the curve
of your spine.

PART II

Though sparsely populated, the Sandhills are nonetheless populated. There are human beings in them there hills, and their confrontations with the environment . . . are the stuff of stories and poems . . . You want poetry? It is everywhere in the speech of those who have made their separate peace, more or less, with the Sandhills.

—William Kloefkorn

JOURNAL

January 13, 1911
No fur in the iron for weeks now, ice
covers the traps, melts and freezes
the jaws open. Nooses
of snares droop like brush
under the weight of snow.

January 18, 1911
The loins of a jackrabbit
were my last meal, days ago.
Fuel scarce, water frozen, the mule's leg
broken, the mule's body bait, wolves
gone to timber. Two shells
in the rifle—one for food,
one for safety.

January ? 1911
I am old. I could have moved
to Omaha years ago. Now what's left
is this journal—as if words
could save me. I lean closer
to the paper, squint into the gray light
and write. Tumbleweeds blow past
the canvas tent-flaps, open
and flapping louder for the wind.
I could eat every word.

DROUGHT

—*Ernest Gotschall, Knox County, Nebraska, 1935*

Bad spring. Dry
cows and steers were first
to go. I kept a pen of pairs
behind the barn, fed them
hay by hand. Then a wave
of grasshoppers swept over
the corn. Now I shove
my pitchfork backwards
into the haypile: just barbs
sticking out, so my sweat
salt won't draw them
to the handle.

*

We'll have to buy more hay to make it
through. The cattle ground
the cornstalks down to nubs.
The pairs behind the barn
I turned out. The grain left
won't feed them. In the coop
I bed nests thin with hay, scatter
a handful of kernels in dust. The hens
will eat well a while. At least
we'll have eggs.

*

I hear there's good land
open in the Sandhills—untouched

by plow, grass enough
for hay, an aquifer below, water
seeping up from springs. I auctioned
the picker and the plow, loaded
furniture in the wagon. Ethel and the boys
will go ahead in the Durant.
Tomorrow, my brother will head
the cattle west. I'll follow
horseback, this hard place
leave behind.

MELVIN

I never saw him limp his antique Ford into town
but once every three weeks or so
for the same two bags of groceries
and a sack of scraps—
for dog food, he would say,
but Lon the butcher said
Hell if Melvin'd waste that meat
feedin' some dog—old boy's probly run outa
jackrabbits to eat or he's pourin' antifreeze on it
for coyote bait.

The guys down at the auto shop told me
Melvin didn't have a telephone
or indoor plumbing in that sod shack,
that when it got too cold to use the outhouse
he'd shit in cardboard boxes
'til they filled, then burn them
in the stove for warmth. He used
dried cow chips instead of wood, they snickered,
though none of them knew because he had
his pickup and tractor parts delivered
to the barbed-wire gate at the end
of his two-mile driveway.

Melvin never married.
Folks said his mom wasn't right in the head, that he
took care of her. When she died they said
it had been the other way around—that's why
he'd never gone to high school in town.
Others whispered he'd been kicked out
of the Army, but after a while they explained
that he was just too old. How old

nobody knew—rumor had it
his dad delivered him on the dirt floor
of the dugout side of a sand hill
he slapped a porch on and called home.

When they found Melvin he'd been dead
for so long the coyotes dragged him off
from where he'd fallen fixing fence,
gloves on his hands,
pliers in his pocket
a half-mile from home, where in the yard
the tractors and hay equipment sat
parked in a straight row, tires lined up
in descending wheelbase length.
In the barn square bales stood stacked
to the rafters, packed to the walls
and corners, a monument
to sweat.

In the house, on the plank floor in the middle
of the main room a cold cook-stove
squatted. Against one wall slouched a worn-
out couch. Along the other rested a white
wooden rocker with the paint worn off the seat,
and when I think about Melvin now
I imagine how he sat there in that chair,
maybe reading a newspaper until he fell asleep
every weekend night for so long
with no one telling him he ought to go
to town for a beer or a ball game, then
for so long with just nobody
but the dog, if he had one, howling
to the coyotes they both
would one day join.

BAIT

When I found her, the ewe
still lived. Her head bloomed
from the place her face had been,
each breath red spume. Throat crushed,
tongue eaten, hind legs chewed
to bone, she made no sound
but a gurgle. I shot her

and dragged the body to where
tracks in snow found sand. Knelt
on a burlap sack, I hacked
frozen ground with a hatchet.
I opened the steel-jawed yawn, nocked
trigger to pan, sifted dry dirt
over top and smoothed it to look
like nothing. Nearby,

on shit flecked with bits of wool
I dripped piss milked
from a coyote bladder.
When I finished, the fat sun
squatted on a hilltop, then
slunk behind, silent. The trap,
nested in its bed, rested,
patient and certain as morning.

Daybreak

Slickered under rain I stand in what was once
a fence-corner, the box-anchor broken,
railroad-ties splintered like shims.
The hackles bristle on the neck

of my dog, whose silence says nothing
but fear—what must have been what drove
the cattle through the barbed wire. I look down

at what remains of the fence, trampled
by hooves into the ground, in the mud
a single cat track bigger than my hand.

Morning sun buds over the rim of cattle-
scattered hills. The rain quits. The dog whines.
My finger traces the edge of the print:
deep, round, and dry.

Osage Orange

My father said *These posts are tougher than nails,*
as he ran his hands along the yellow-ruckled wood.

I'll understand what he meant, when
after a few years and my shoulders have grown

I'm strong enough to work the post-hole diggers,
because I'll have to splice the wire the cows broke.

I'll bend all of the staples over twice
before I get them pounded back in.

*

Before I get them pounded back in,
I'll bend all of the staples over twice

because I'll have to splice the wire the cows broke.
I'm strong enough to work the post-hole diggers

after a few years, and my shoulders have grown.
I'll understand what he meant, when

as he ran his hands along the yellow-ruckled wood,
my father said *These posts are tougher than nails.*

MAD COW

—*Holt County, Nebraska*

One time there was this black white-
faced cow got into the shelterbelt
and wouldn't come out. I let
the fence down but she just kept
running back and forth through
the cedars. My dogs couldn't even
get her run out of there. So I took
my lariat and tied one end of it
to the pickup. The other end I ran
under the wires of the fence I'd stapled up
and laid the noose across where she'd
tromped a path. Sure enough, that cow
come down that same trail and got caught
by two back feet. I jerked the slack and
the wife gunned it. Pulled her right under
the wire and out of those trees—and another
quarter-mile away. That cow's old head
swung back and forth like she couldn't
figure out what the hell was happening.
She was pretty upset about it, even after
I turned her loose. The wife and I
got a kick out of that.

THE BLIND JERSEY

She hears the plastic spool squeak
as I crank the handle to roll back
the electric wire. Marbled eyes
wide and alert, she stops

at the edge of short and tall, as though
the fence still holds her. Blinking,
she reaches, head sideways, and frogs
a tongue of clover. She chews, considers,
then blows snot and bounds past

like a calf, like she hasn't done this
every day, as if she has remembered,
or better yet forgotten, if she ever knew,
just what it could have been
to see.

HORSE TRADE

That scar on his nose he got
running smack into a barb-
wire fence when he was a colt,
but he's a real good mover,
never offered to buck.

Reminds me of a dun gelding
Harvey Maxwell used to rope feet on.
Only heeling horse he ever had. Old Harv
liked his whiskey a little too much, but that dun
knew just what to do, so he always gave Harv
a pretty good shot.

My drinkin' days are over, but I still
play a hand every now and again.
The good Lord blessed me
with a heck of a wife
who don't squawk too much
when I come home late
after a tough game.

Like I say, this one's never offered to buck,
but I haven't pushed him too hard,
so I don't know what he'll do
when you start to working on his mind.
Just stay out of his face
and you should get along fine.

DOWNER

Kneeling on frozen manure, the dry cow
struggles and fails to stand, hind ankles bent
in nerve-damaged curls. I place alfalfa
at one shoulder, at the other, a pan half-
full of soy hulls. She will not survive
labor, but cutting out the calf soon
could save it. From the well I bucket water,
trying not to slosh it onto my leg.
She drinks deep, shivers with the chill,
closes her eyes, tucks her head against her ribs
and sleeps. The body within
fights each breath's frosted cloud
with all its might.

RESOLUTION

—January at the Roundup Bar, Atkinson, Nebraska

Somebody's bull must have jumped the fence
early. The fall yearling heifers
plumped up
then started going down.

Must have been a big old Saler bull
because when I cut the heads off
to get them to come out,
every god-damned one of them
was red as the devil's own.

If the calves made it
the mothers didn't—
never both—the little bastards froze their ears
and tails off by the time
I found them, and sometimes
they were just blood, hair
and coyote shit in the snow.

Sure was one hell of a god-damned way
to start off the new year.
Sure did make it tough to quit whiskey
like I told myself I would.
Tell you one thing, though,
I've had it with ranching
and that's a promise. Say,
how about another?
I'm almost empty here.

TORNADO

The dark cloud funneled down
six miles southeast of town and followed
sand river-banks, paying no mind
to square section lines or straight roads.
It scattered bales, windmills, pen-panels
and outbuildings until the hills
and meadows looked misplaced.

Angus steers hung like trash bags
on irrigation pivots, brood mares
tossed across the road squirmed
broken-backed in tall grass, hobbled
on two or three legs, and cried up
to their weanling colts
impaled on cottonwood branches,
their screams all silenced
by the muffled reports
of gunshots.

Weeks later, the fences clipped off
neat as rows of roses along the river road
were rebuilt, staples pounded flush
into the flesh of fresh cedar posts,
barbed wire tight and shiny
as new belts. Squared pastures
stood empty, grass tall
and waiting after rain.

All there was left to do
was find, gather, replace,
keep both feet on the ground
and at least one eye

on the bigger than Big Sky sky so big
even it saw that one coming
but couldn't do anything
but stay in the way and watch.

Smoke

I saw it on the way back
from the field, where
I raked hay with a cabless tractor,
the upright muffler's exhaust
against my face cooler
than the wind blowing hard
across the hills' baked sand.

When I got home Dad had the cream-
can loaded full of water and burlap sacks
in the back of the Chevy.
Going 70 on the gravel, he hit the brakes
and slid toward the ditch, slowing
to miss barn swallows diving
low across the road to pick gnats
from the hot air.

I opened barbed-wire gates
into one neighbor's pasture
after another, squeezing them shut
fast enough only to still feel slower
than the wide wall rising between drought-
brown grass and the sun.

FIRE

After the tanker trucks have gone back for more,
a furrow darkens the windward side
of swirling ash. Next to pickups
in an uneven row, neighbors stand in soot-
stained clothes, rags tied around
mouths and noses, arms resting on cream-
can rims, hands clutching
wet burlap sacks, waiting

for grass-roots to flare, ready
to beat the flames back
into the earth, down
to where they spring
like water—water which once covered
this ocean of grass—water
unable to save even this one
small part from burning.

GRASSHOPPERS

They arrive overnight
from nowhere, fallen angels
crawling everywhere, mandibles
scouring fence posts as if
to devour bare wood.

Each destroys ten times
what it eats, the choicest morsels
of tender green shoots, until pastures
lie in ruin. Cattle ship out
to feedlots to eat grain
like birds and coyotes glut
grasshoppers, more
than they can hold.

The creeks sink deeper
into their beds. Burning wind
blows sand in a slow, steady casting-
out of the brittle hills. The rancher
turns his face to the sky. Wrinkles
crease his forehead like shadows
of barbed wire across bare,
inedible ground. He prays

for mercy's cool drops to fall. Afternoons,
clouds gather, bellies brown
and swollen. From them
a darkness descends, the air alive
with flight. They light
on fences, in trees. Evenings moan
a death-song of wings.

60

ON THE KILL FLOOR

There, as I stood in the hide-
humid air, the smell of fresh fat sharp
as a stick-knife, blood swirled
like hair down the drain
at my feet, where a calf spilled out
with the guts of its mother
before my bone-saw split her.

How whole it looked—tiny hooves,
ears and tail well-formed, nose no bigger
than a thimble, like rubber, lashes
long on the never-lifted lids.
I tossed it on the pile of severed heads,
their eyes open and dull
as stones, then turned back
to the business of bones.

SHARPENING SICKLES

The rusty rows of triangles lie
like dinosaur tails on the shop floor.
One by one I raise the bars
to the workbench, then clamp
their spines in the vise.
My file's rough tongue licks
their faces to shines.

Every pitted edge recalls
some youthful sharpness, each loose rivet
snugs to itself like a hug. To have
the resolve of steel, I think—to keep
a temper so solid, so keen, so as to slice
neat through nearly any met thing—
to hold fast to form with such mettle.

When the heat my task makes
raises drops on my forehead, I stop.
I open the overhead doors and step
into the bright day, a light breeze
cool across my face. Grass, waist-
high and fragrant, stands waving,
wind-rippled, in far fields.

Old Barn

You see it off the road a ways, its peeling paint
nearly hidden by a copse of cottonwoods, the lane
leading in overgrown, the gate rusted shut.

You park on the shoulder, cross the ditch and step over
the sagging barbed wire fence into the stackyard,
molding leftover haypiles like bison humps.

You almost trip on the harrow near the door, hidden
by thistles, their spine-stems bursting, bird-planted,
from cowchips caught in its broken teeth years ago.

The walls lean inward, upheld only by corners,
the concave roof a caution. Inside, blink to dim dark,
nail-holes like stars in the tin overhead. A sparrow perches

on the leg of an upturned milkstool. Bundles of bale-twine,
salt-sacks and stacks of sickle-sections crowd a crooked shelf,
the stall's bedding peppered with droppings. Before you leave,

you want to take a picture, but you forgot your camera.
Driving away, you look back one last time at the old barn, alone,
its gambrel roof like shoulders, shrugging, leaf-dappled in sun.

Part III

These Nebraska skies,
they hold me like a mother
and they bring a promise
with their morning light.
Like a song
that is brother to your stories,
they'll cradle you
in your longest night.
And they will be with you
in your longest night.

Out here
This old wind's been known to blow.
Some nights so cold
You think they will not end.
It leaves you looking round
for some old storyteller
who'll lead you first to home
and back again.
And you want to go home
and then come back again.

—John Walker

RIDING TO WORK

On this 30-degree May Thursday morning
the buckskin's ears point south
into a southwest gust.
Ten miles from the bunkhouse
to the arena, in an hour
I'll be to work, although in fact
I'm working now, getting one ridden
before I get there,
where more horses wait,
eating alfalfa flakes in their stalls.

I follow fenced edges of pastures
summer grazed and fall fallow, cornfields
stubbled, irrigation-pivots still in the wind.
I tighten my hat-string under my chin, warm
in a flannel coat and chaps, loping
graveled two-tracks on Kea,
Lakota for *frog*, his owner said,
an apt name as he shies at a rooster-
pheasant's ratcheting alarm, snorts
and almost hops from under me.

I watch for badger holes,
their dark mouths waiting
to swallow my horse's shins,
weave between low-hanging
cottonwood branches and cedars.
His breath growing shorter, Kea settles
into long-trot, his black legs eating
the ground, my body rocking
in the saddle seat, leather
creaking, the latigo sweat-stained.

In the quiet between gusts,
mourning doves murmur
and pick kernels of gravel from the sand
the gelding's hooves sink into, steel shoes
clinking an occasional stone.
As the sun breaks, meadowlarks stretch
wings above barbed wire. I guide
the buckskin west, pink sky behind us
as we descend the slope of hills
into the last valley.

Along the county road now, Kea's neck
steaming in the sun-warming air, I wave
at a Suburban, a man driving alone.
I wonder what he's thinking, warm
in the car seat while my ass tingles
from denim on leather, my feet
in stirrups instead of pressing pedals.
He glances at me as he passes,
smiles, raises a single finger
from inefficiency's expensive wheel,

and we meet like this,
riding to work, a speed-limit sign
between us growing smaller in his rear-
view mirror and over my shoulder.
The arena not far now,
Kea's pace quickens—a clean stall,
water and hay ahead of him, the scent
of other horses pulling him
like the rest of us
into the wind.

CALF ROPER

My younger brother Marcus backs
his sorrel calf horse Droopy into the box, and stands
in the stirrups, piggin string between his teeth. He leans
over the pommel, and takes a couple practice swings.
Every muscle in the horse's neck is flexed,
veins bulging and ready to explode,
every fibril quivering with pause,
bloodshot eyes unblinking as he waits

for the boot-heel tap that comes
after my brother nods like a surgeon
before the first incision.
This look I have seen
in the practice pen, right before
he lays back the barrier and tracks one down
if he has to, a look I have seen
just before he two-swings the loop,
sticks a fat knot smack on top
of the calf's head with the slack dismounts,

which he does now—left hand sliding rope,
legs pumping in the arena sand—as the horse
sits and the calf hits the end, flips
and gets up winded. Marcus flanks him
easy as folding up a chair, straddles,
strings, two-wraps and a half-hitch
tight, hands in the air
before the dust clears.

Droopy works rope, keeping back
like he's getting paid. Marcus gathers
the jerk-line, hurries calm

back to the horse, mounts slow
to wait for the six-second count.
When the judge's flag drops, the announcer shouts
the time, and I know how high
my brother is by the way he rides out,
head cocked back under his black felt hat, that he knows
what he's done. The blisters on his fingers
don't matter, and neither do bruises

on my feet and legs from pushing calves for him.
I've forgotten hours on the road
burning diesel, listening to the same songs
on the radio, and it's worth
greasy cook-shack burgers and long nights
in the tent under hard rain,

because Marcus and I are drunk
on the silence precision and speed,
and the cries of the cowgirls in the bleachers
who might love my brother as much as I do,
make me understand for a moment
why he's a calf roper, why I
like to watch him
like it's me out there—
doing it *just so* and *'cause I can*—
doing it
just like that.

SOMEWHERE IN NEBRASKA

I picture her horseback, one leg hooked
over the saddle horn as she watched
team roping. Hat-brim tipped
low across her eyes, she chewed sunflower-
seeds and spit the shells
at my boots. I don't remember

which rodeo, or the color
of her horse, hat, or eyes.
I'm sure the heeler caught
both feet, because when he did
she looked at me, winked, and said
Throwing a heel loop's a lot like sex—
once you get the tip in the rest is easy.

It was June or July—I forget,
but there was heat,
her unbuttoned shirt's V
and the rivulet a bead of sweat left
as it slipped along a curve of breast
when she leaned down to offer me

a handful of sunflower seeds. In my mind
her neck was tan, the shirt
sky, its buttons
pearl, but her phone number
scribbled on a rodeo-
program's torn-off corner

I can't recall. This I know: the day's heat
shaded into evening. That night
from the rise above the river, we could see

across the Sandhills. The lights
of some distant town glowed golden
like the firelight on her skin. Her hands
were small and strong, her mouth
whiskey-warm. Her hair against my face
whispered *woodsmoke, alfalfa,*
dust.

TEARING OUT FENCE

Gripping the tractor loader, my free hand wraps
a 12-foot fence post with log chain I hook
to itself. I drop. Squints mans the levers,
raises the loader, tightens the chain until
its links bite wood. The ground groans loose
the post, ringed with sod, leaving
yawning a hole I fill
pushing sand with my boot.

Squints lowers the post. The chain falls
undone. I move to the next one. My brother
walks behind, bends to bear-hug each log. Standing,
he stacks them on the trailer neat
as toothpicks, packing them like shoes
in a suitcase, swapping wide and narrow ends
so they don't roll. When he tires
we switch. I walk,

the sun high and hot. Shadows
on surrounding hills disappear
with dew on grazed bluestem blades. I gaze
into thousands of acres from horizon
to cottonwoods, whose broad leaves swivel
in shades of distant space. A band
of bison browses by. A cow separates,
comes closer,
curious. Her winter coat
hangs ragged, drags the ground, her horns
like horse ears.

She stands,
observing me, my skin red against
the fence, behind me a pock-
marked line of craters. She watches
the boundary go, the glow in her eyes
her smile at me, grunting
one post after another, scrawny,
sunburned, sweaty, owing her
at least as much
and knowing.

COUNTRY MUSIC

After the rodeo, after the slack, after
barbecues and whiskey come out
to warm bellies against the night air,
a down-on-his-luck roper sits
on a haybale next to a trailer, picks
a beat-up guitar and sings
to no one in particular:
Bobbled my tie in Billings, drew
the pup in Lusk and missed. Kissed
a girl in Ogallala, split my lip
on her boyfriend's fist.

On a drive, cowboys whistle and yell
Hike cow, git up in there now, at cattle
whose hooves strike rhythms syncopated
to horses stepping. Saddles creak,
ropes rattle, loops swing their wind-
song with the march fife
of a meadowlark.

Cold spring mornings,
the cow-camp cook sings
Wake up, Jacob
Day's a-breakin'
Sun's comin' up and the moon is gone
Bacon in the pan, coffee in the pot
Wake up now, Jacob, get it while it's hot.

Later, fresh-cut testicles sizzle
over the roaring furnace, the clink
of red-hot irons cues calves calling,
their mothers responding, all bawling

through the barbed wire night
into the day, and so on, until
at last the first one stops,
breathes deep, lips to grass,
and the silence of the prairie
takes to the wean.

LARK

There must have been a spot
on the floor of the Sistine Chapel
where Michelangelo stood to look up,
just as Da Vinci had an angle
from a place
from which he first saw
the Mona Lisa's sad smile,
where light met eye, where texture,
shadow and color became life.

Trying to find a place like that today
at the Art Institute in Chicago
in front of Jules Breton's *Song of the Lark*,
I stand ten feet back and to the left,
and as my eyes stray from focus,
the borders between colors
disappear, the rising sun melts
into the canvas sky,
and clarity returns

as the barefoot peasant girl,
rag around her head,
scythe in her hand,
steps toward me, pauses,
one foot forward, and stands
right here in this field
as the morning songbird warbles
its call into the chill of dawn,
and all at once,

Antonia Shimerda wades through the tall-
grass prairie toward the meeting-place,

my great-grandmother Carlson sweeps
the slat porch of a clapboard farmhouse
somewhere between Crofton and Wausa, Nebraska,
and my mother finishes the morning milking,
turns the last cow out to pasture and whispers
a prayer to the disappearing stars,

and all three become the first girl
I ever loved
in the first harvest season
of our lives together.
She is about to say something to me
but stops instead to hear
the song kissing her ears
and mine.

MIDNIGHT

The moon is a thumb-
nail clipping tonight, the top
rails of the corral cribbed
thin as wrists
by the colt, who stands
hipshot, stomping gray dust
into a rising curtain

as millers crowd
the bare bulb atop
a slanted pine pole,
around which circle
two tomcats, claws drawn,
each staring down the fight
reflected in the other's eyes.

Team Roping

In the afternoon heat
a spring wind blows
sand through the arena
as the header
spins a steer. My brother,
heeling, ropes two feet
and wraps the saddle-
horn twice.

Though he'll tell me later
he didn't feel the coil slip
over his wrist, now
when he stops his horse
to draw the slack tight,
the rope slides
through the skin-
nerves and bone-
meat of his right thumb
as the flag drops
on a round-winning
six-second run.

He dismounts,
gathers his rope
one loop
after another, hangs it
on the horn, pats
his horse's neck
and leads the sorrel gelding
to the fence, where he ties him
and looks at the crowd
staring, then

peels off his dirty-
white cotton glove. Inside,

the thumb dangles
by a floss-thin
ligament, pale
strung to purple
like past
and future
now thrust together
into a bag of melting ice.

The Same Road My Father Drove

On my last errand of summer
before I go west
and leave my father
to milk mornings
and wonder
whether to borrow and build
or sell out and start again,
knowing no one might come back
to help or take over the ranch, I drive

the same '69 Chevy pickup
as he did, its red paint faded
a tired orange,
and navigate the washboards
of this unpaved road,
still the same, save
for a layer of gravel put down
and power lines put up
less than twenty years before.

The Chevy rumbles
across the auto gate at Herrington's.
Hereford cattle stand
ass-end to the sun,
sidestep, chew cud,
button-eyed calves run
into the ditch mud
to stop and stare, flag
the air with white-tipped tails.

Here there are fewer people than cows,
fewer people even now

than then,
when he would have been
driving past the Mill Iron V ranch house
where the girlfriend before my mother lived,
now a leaning, slatted shell
of peeled-away paint-speckled gray boards,
an early calving season cow camp.

He would be driving to meet her—
my mom, not the girlfriend—
at the clinic on Panzer Street
in Newport, where she, seventeen
and as many weeks pregnant,
would come out and sit next to him
on the Chevy's front bench seat
and ride to Bassett to eat
lunch at the Range Café,

where today I share a corner booth
with a burger and a mound of potato salad,
talk to Doc White, the retired vet,
filling up his day with cups
of weak coffee and overheard gossip.
He looks at me
as my father sometimes does
when he asks if I've heard the story
to match the scar.

Doc tips a finger to his toothpick,
says, *Watch you don't hang a spur,*
and smiles as I walk out
to the Chevy he's seen driving
the same road my father drove
miles before, headed south
to where the crumbled correction-line

meets the gravel
a half-mile past Green Valley Sunday School.

I pass the old Tasler place that someone
with a woman to help him could fix up
and fill with children, surrounded
by stirrup-high bluestem and brome enough
to graze pairs and put up hay for winter,
then the one-room schoolhouse,
where kids play kickball in a pasture,
the dust kicked up by the tires of the Chevy
filtered through their laughter.

Rolling past the red D2 Ranch barn,
where Bruce's three beautiful cowgirl daughters
rope breakaway calves in the arena,
I wave, driving the same road my father drove
to bring his newly-wed teenage bride
and their son,
my brother,
the first of five
to the shelterbelt and the home place,

where I turn in, park
and shut off the Chevy,
returning for today,
not to stay but having driven
the same road my father drove, which,
leading me here, can't help
but lead me away
to other things just as beautiful
and useless.

MONTANA

The day wasn't exactly a woman
who loved me, but I was with one. Why
we were drawn together made as much
sense as did our reason for leaving
Nebraska behind. When we left
Spearfish at sunrise

I drove her Buick and knew
we could never go back. The Black
Hills faded to gray, cheap gas at a truck stop
in Wyoming, then Powder River country,
the Little Big Horn, like Wounded Knee,
another last stand. I was running

from a thousand acres of blood, she
from her husband, her life
like mine, about to change. About
what we hoped to find, I can say little. No,
nothing. Little to nothing changed
anyway, not even after a night

in Bozeman, three in Missoula, the balcony
overlooking the Clark Fork where she smoked
naked afterward. When it was all over
we didn't want anyone to know. At least
no one who didn't already. Already
we could see how we would fail, how
it would never be over. A week later

she drove back alone. The car that brought me
ended up on its top in the Colorado. I called to find,
a day after she got out, she was fine. That night

I slept in an Idaho basement, cold
leaking in through the window overhead
like river water, the bed
barely big enough for one.

IDAHO

For the promise of two-fifty a week
I ride horses and doctor calves
while the grass in Nebraska is tall
as a horseback man's knee
and growing, rain needed for years
falling, Holt Creek's banks overflowing,
cattle ripening on hillsides.

Unable to calm the black mare, yet miles
from her tiring, I ride circles
as another calf, scoured,
skeletal, insides parched,
drops to his knees
and with a swollen tongue
laps at the dust.

Searching for the withered vein,
my fingers tremble as I jab his neck yet again
with the needle, each bloodless thrust
an empty promise
until one thick drop beads purple.
I raise the plastic fluid bag
to start the drip.

The black mare watches me,
wide-eyed, untrusting
after what someone else did to her sometime,
and I don't want to swing into that borrowed saddle.
It doesn't fit either one of us
and my ass is sore, but for walking
these boots aren't much good.

I look to the east. The sun climbs above
Treasure Valley, where it seems nothing
not watered by the hand of man grows.
Last summer's drought,
yearling brother to this newborn season,
feels like yesterday, and Nebraska waits,
only Wyoming away.

NOTES

p.xi, Epigraph 1
Johnsgard, Paul. *The Nature of Nebraska*. Lincoln: University of Nebraska, 2001, p.77.

p.xi, Epigraph 2
Sandoz, Mari. *The Cattlemen*. Lincoln, University of Nebraska: 1958, pp.427-8.

p.15, Epigraph
Roethke, Theodore. "The Far Field." From Ramanzani, Jahan; Ellman, Richard; and O'Clair, Robert, *The Norton Anthology of Modern and Contemporary Poetry*. Third Edition, Vol.1. New York: Norton, 2003, p.854.

p.24, Epigraph, "Heat"
Bierds, Linda. "Safe." *The Profile Makers*. New York: Henry Holt, 1997, p.57.

p.25, Epigraph, "Hayfield, late July"
Stafford, William. "Haycutters." *The Way It Is: New and Selected Poems*. St. Paul, Minnesota: Graywolf, 1998, p.42.

p.41, Epigraph
Kloefkorn, William. "The Poetry of People and Place," keynote address presented at the Mari Sandoz Heritage Society Annual Conference, April 14, 2005. Published by the Mari Sandoz Heritage Society and the Nebraska Lottery, 2006, pp.15,18.

p.44, Epigraph, "Drought"
Ernest Gotschall, my great-grandfather, was a sharecropper in Knox County, Nebraska, until the Dust Bowl, when he and his family packed up their belongings and drove over 100 cattle over 150 miles to Holt County, where he purchased (on almost

unheard of and ridiculously generous handshake credit) the
ranch where I grew up.

p.50, "Osage Orange"

The idea for this poem's form was derived from an assignment
given by Natasha Trethewey during the Fall 2006 University of
Idaho Distinguished Visiting Writers workshop. The palindrome
form is based on the poem "Myth" in her book *Native Guard.*

p.65, Epigraph

Walker, John. "Nebraska Skies." *John Walker: from Okie Boy to the
Loup River.* Lincoln, Nebraska: Prairie Dog Music, 2005. Album
liner notes, pp.42-3.

p.82, "The Same Road My Father Drove"

The road referred to by the title and subsequent lines in this
poem is 468th Avenue, and runs south from Holt County road
#870 through my family's ranch, then cuts west, crosses the
Holt/Rock county line and turns back north, intersecting U.S.
Highway 20 at Spring Valley Park near Newport, Nebraska.

Printed in the United States
133391LV00001B/289-312/P